THE BIG BANG
EXPLAINED

THE
MYSTERIES
OF
SPACE

THE BIG BANG
EXPLAINED

MEGAN ANSDELL

Enslow Publishing
101 W. 23rd Street
Suite 240
New York, NY 10011
USA

enslow.com

Published in 2019 by Enslow Publishing, LLC.
101 W. 23rd Street, Suite 240, New York, NY 10011

Library of Congress Cataloging-in-Publication Data

Names: Ansdell, Megan, author.
Title: The Big Bang explained / Megan Ansdell.
Description: New York : Enslow Publishing, LLC, [2019] | Series: The
mysteries of space | Audience: Grades 7 to 12. | Includes bibliographical
references and index.
Identifiers: LCCN 2017055587| ISBN 9780766099562 (library bound) | ISBN
9780766099579 (pbk.)
Subjects: LCSH: Big bang theory—Juvenile literature. | Expanding
universe—Juvenile literature. | Cosmology—Juvenile literature. | Hubble,
Edwin, 1889–1953—Juvenile literature.
Classification: LCC QB991.B54 A57 2018 | DDC 523.1/8—dc23
LC record available at https://lccn.loc.gov/2017055587

Printed in the United States of America

To Our Readers: We have done our best to make sure all website addresses in this
book were active and appropriate when we went to press. However, the author and
the publisher have no control over and assume no liability for the material available
on those websites or on any websites they may link to. Any comments or
suggestions can be sent by email to customerservice@enslow.com.

Photos Credits: Cover Vadim Sadovski/Shutterstock.com; pp. 6-7 sripfoto/
Shutterstock.com; p. 11 Hulton Deutsch/Corbis Historical/Getty Images; p. 13 ALXR/
Shutterstock.com; p. 17 generalfmv/Shutterstock.com; p. 18 Andrea Danti/
Shutterstock.com; p. 22, 31 adapted from diagrams provided by the author; p. 25
Robin Treadwell/Science Source; p. 27 Science Source/Getty Images; pp. 28-29,
66-67 NASA/Hulton Archive/Getty Images; p. 33 David Parker/Science Source; p. 38
Science History Images/Alamy Stock Photo; pp. 40, 52 NASA/Science Source; p. 43
Library of Congress Prints and Photographs Division; pp. 46-47 Pozdeyev Vitaly
/Shutterstock.com; p. 54 NASA 382199/Corbis News/Getty Images; p. 58 Mark
Garlick/Science Source; p. 61 Take 27 Ltd/Science Source; p. 63 Xinhua/Alamy
Stock Photo; p. 64 Crystal Eye Studio/Shutterstock.com; back cover and interior
pages sdecoret/Shutterstock.com (earth's atmosphere from space), clearviewstock
/Shutterstock.com (space and stars).

CONTENTS

The universe is nearly fourteen billion years old, and today it is filled with roughly one hundred billion galaxies, each of which contain about one hundred billion stars. Each of these stars likely hosts a planetary system similar to the solar system. The planet Earth orbits a fairly average star known as the sun, which formed about 4.6 billion years ago in the outskirts of a spiral galaxy, known as the Milky Way. But how did these structures in the universe form, and from where did the matter that they are made of come? To answer these questions, we must go back to the beginning of the universe, when matter and energy were created, and follow their evolution into the universe seen today.

The cosmological model that describes the very beginning of the universe is known as the big bang theory. The big bang starts off with a universe that is infinitely small and dense, representing the beginning

This is our Milky Way galaxy as it is seen today, nearly 14 billion years after the Big Bang.

of time itself. In the moments that follow, the universe rapidly expands; this expansion lowers the density and temperature of space, allowing the earliest atomic nuclei of hydrogen and helium to form within just the first few minutes of the universe's existence. Galaxies are created roughly one billion years later, and as space continues to expand and cool, the universe as it is seen today forms.

How is it possible to study the origin of the universe? Indeed, astronomers cannot directly observe the birth of the universe to confirm the initial conditions that are predicted by the big bang theory. But good scientific theories not only provide descriptions of the physical world based on the laws of physics, they also provide testable predictions that can be confirmed through observations. The big bang theory is widely accepted by modern cosmologists, because it makes concrete predictions about the observable universe, which have been tested repeatedly with striking success.

Chapter One

The Beginning of the Beginning

The story of the birth and evolution of the universe can be divided into several key time periods, or epochs, each defined by fundamental changes in the physical conditions of the universe. A lot happens within just the first fractions of a second of the universe's existence. The universe begins as an infinitely small and dense collection of matter and radiation, then rapidly expands and cools, drastically changing its physical state. During these first moments, the fundamental forces, such as gravity and electromagnetic force, are also established.

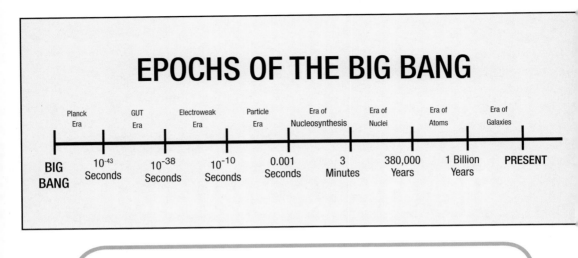

These are the key time periods, or epochs, of the Big Bang.

Planck Epoch

The first 10^{-43} seconds after the big bang (where 10^{-43} is scientific notation for an extremely tiny fraction) is known as the Planck Epoch, after the German physicist Max Planck (1858–1947), one of the founders of quantum mechanics.[1] During this inconceivably short period of time, the universe is an infinitesimally (or extremely) small collection of matter and radiation. The densities and temperatures are so extreme (nearly infinite) that our current understanding of physics is unable to explain the physical conditions of the universe at this time. One of the difficulties with explaining the physical conditions of the universe during the Planck Epoch is that it requires linking quantum mechanics (the theory for describing the universe across very small-scale structures, such as atomic nuclei) with general relativity (the theory for describing the universe across large-scale structures,

Max Planck (1858–1947) was a German physicist who won the Nobel Prize in 1918 for his foundational work on quantum theory.

such as stars and galaxies). Physicists one day hope to merge these theories into a single unified theory called quantum gravity.

Grand Unified Theory (GUT) Epoch

To understand the next epoch of the big bang, it is important to know that everything in the current universe is governed by four distinct forces: gravitational force, electromagnetic force, weak nuclear force, and strong nuclear force. Gravity is the force that is most familiar because it is the "glue" that keeps together the things seen in everyday life (such as one's feet to the ground and Earth orbiting around the sun). Gravity is actually the weakest force, but it operates across large distances and depends on mass, a tangible quantity. The electromagnetic force is perhaps the next most familiar force: it operates over the same distances as gravity, but is much stronger, and as the name implies, it depends on electrical charge (rather than mass). Many large objects are electrically neutral because positive and negative charges cancel each other out, but on a small scale the electromagnetic force plays an important role in holding atoms and molecules together. The strong nuclear force and weak nuclear force only operate over the extremely short distances within atomic nuclei. The strong force is the strongest of the fundamental forces and binds atomic nuclei together, while the weak force is most important for radioactive decay (in particular beta decay).

Under the extreme temperatures and densities that characterize the very beginnings of the universe, three of these four fundamental forces were likely combined into one unified force. To understand how the fundamental forces could be united, a useful analogy is the different phases of water (ice,

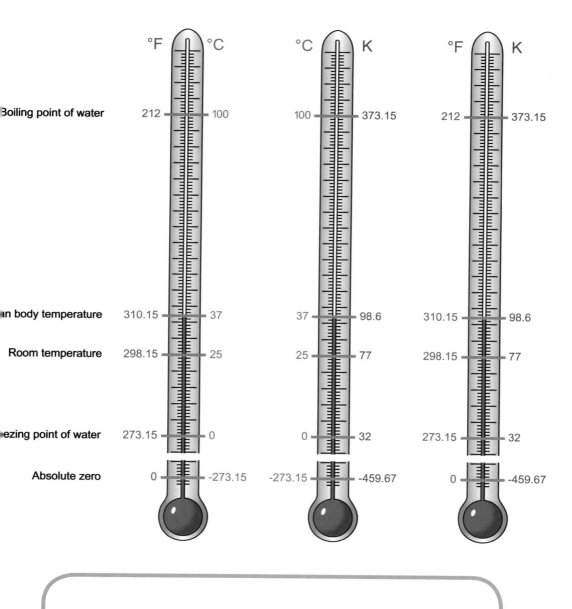

These thermometers compare the Fahrenheit, Celsius, and Kelvin temperature scales.

liquid, steam): these substances are all made of the same molecule (H_2O) but appear as different forms under the right conditions. The Grand Unified Theories (GUTs) describe this merging of the electromagnetic, strong nuclear, and weak nuclear forces into a single force (gravity may have separated earlier during the Planck Era, although we cannot explain this based on the current understanding of physics). During this so-called GUT Epoch, the universe is an inconceivably tiny fraction of a second old (10^{-43} to 10^{-38} s) and is roughly the size of an atomic nucleus, with temperatures reaching a mind-boggling 10^{30} Kelvin (K). Scientists use Kelvin to describe temperature, rather than Fahrenheit or Centigrade, because Kelvin is a true unit of temperature based on "absolute zero."[2] The temperature 0 K is equivalent to -460°F or -273°C. Thus the difference between Kelvin, Celsius, and Fahrenheit temperature scales is negligible compared to the very high temperatures that characterized the early universe.

The GUT Epoch ends when the universe is sufficiently cooled (10^{29} K) for the strong nuclear force to separate from the GUT force, leaving three fundamental forces: gravitational force, strong nuclear force, and still-combined electroweak force. The freezing out of the strong force may also release an enormous amount of energy, triggering an event called inflation, which is the rapid expansion of the universe from the size of an atomic nucleus to the size of the solar system in just 10^{-36} seconds (other models can also explain inflation without a GUT phase transition). Although inflation sounds bizarre, it is one of the best explanations for several key features of the universe, which are otherwise difficult to explain.

Electroweak Epoch

The next time period of the big bang is known as the Electroweak Epoch, named because the electromagnetic and weak nuclear forces are still unified, while the gravitational and strong forces are separated. During this time, the universe is a hot and dense sea of radiation (massless packets of light energy, known as photons) rapidly converting back and forth into matter (objects with mass, such as electrons) through a process called annihilation.

It may sound strange that mass and energy can convert back and forth, but this is just a consequence of Einstein's famous formula $E=mc^2$, where E is the energy of an object of mass m and c is the speed of light. This formula means that, under the right conditions (such as the high densities and temperatures of the early universe), energy can become mass and vice versa. In particular, when two very energetic photons collide, they can create a particle of matter and its antiparticle. Then, when a particle and its antiparticle collide, they annihilate each other, transforming their mass-energy entirely back into photon-energy.

During the Electroweak Epoch, the creation and destruction of particle-antiparticle pairs occurs in quick succession, such that the total number of particles and photons in the universe is nearly equal. As the universe continues to expand during this time period, it becomes cooler and less dense. The reason why the temperature of the universe drops as it expands is because space itself is expanding: the expansion of space stretches out the wavelengths of radiation and decreases the speeds of particles, which in turn decreases their energies and thus temperatures (recall that temperature is just a measure of average energy). When the universe is about 10^{-10} seconds old, the temperature drops to 10^{15} K, at which point the electromagnetic and weak forces separate, creating the four distinct forces that we know today.

ANTIPARTICLES AND ANNIHILATION

All types of particles have corresponding antiparticles. Particles and antiparticles have the same mass and differ only in their electric charge. One example of a particle-antiparticle pair is an electron and an antielectron (also known as a positron). When particles and antiparticles collide, they destroy each other and form two high-energy photons (known as gamma rays) in a process called annihilation. This process follows Einstein's famous equation $E=mc^2$, which states that matter and radiation are interchangeable. If a photon has an energy that is higher than the E associated with a particle of mass m, then when it collides with a similar photon the result will be the production of a particle-antiparticle pair through a process known as pair production. In the extreme temperatures of the early universe, high-energy photons were common, and so photons and matter rapidly converted back and forth via annihilation and pair production.

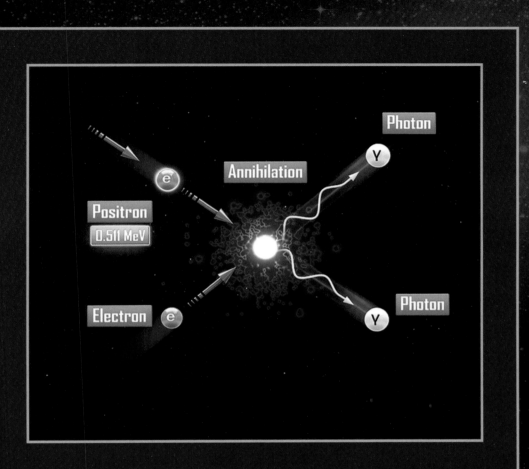

Two photons form from a particle and antiparticle pair through the process of annihilation.

As the universe expanded and cooled, high-energy photons became rare, which meant that pair production was no longer possible. At this point, all the particles annihilated their antiparticle pairs. Fortunately, particles outnumbered antiparticles in the early universe, which meant that some matter was left over to make stars, galaxies, and eventually even humans.

Particle Epoch

During the Particle Epoch, the universe continues to expand and cool. At an age of one millisecond, the temperature drops to 10^{12} K. Under these relatively cooler conditions (still over one hundred million times hotter than the surface of the sun), the universe is no longer hot enough for photons and matter to easily

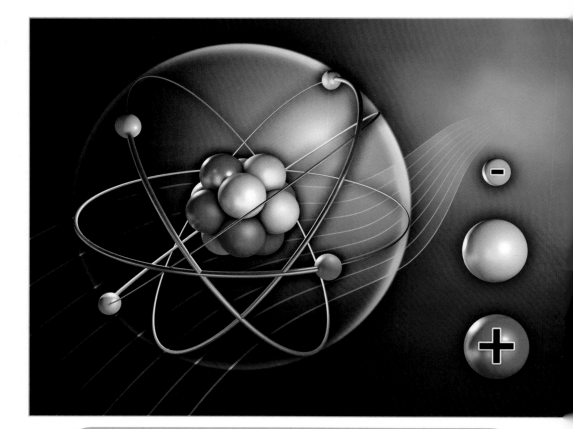

Atoms are made up of three kinds of particles: electrons (the blue, negatively charged balls), protons (the red, positively charged balls), and neutrons (the white, neutral balls). Note that this image is not to scale.

exchange back and forth via annihilation and pair production. Consequently, all of the particle-antiparticle pairs annihilate each other and photons become the dominant source of energy in the universe.

For reasons that remain unknown, there were slightly more particles than antiparticles in the early universe. This means that after all of the particle-antiparticle pairs annihilated each other during the Particle Epoch, all of the antiparticles were destroyed, but some particles still remained. This is a very fortunate event, as these leftover particles make up all of the recognizable matter in the present universe—including you! At the end of the Particle Epoch, matter was mostly in the form of protons, neutrons, and electrons—the familiar particles that make up atoms—as well as neutrinos (another elementary particle that is less familiar because it has a near-zero mass and is electrically neutral).

Chapter Two

From Protons to Galaxies

Just one second after the big bang, the first nuclei of hydrogen and helium form from protons and neutrons, creating a universe that begins to look a little more familiar to us. It is then several hundred thousand years before the universe is cool enough to allow neutral atoms and, eventually, stars to form. At roughly one billion years of age, the galaxies as they appear today finally begin to take shape.

Nucleosynthesis Epoch

Nucleosynthesis is the process of forming atomic nuclei from protons and neutrons, which together are known as nucleons. For protons and neutrons to fuse into atomic nuclei, they must be energetic enough and close enough for the attraction of the strong nuclear force to overwhelm the repulsiveness of the electromagnetic force. This process is known as overcoming the Coulomb Barrier. During the Nucleosynthesis Epoch, the densities and temperatures of the universe are still high enough that nucleons can overcome the Coulomb Barrier and fuse into atomic nuclei.

However, high-energy photons are also still common early in the Nucleosynthesis Epoch. As a result, the atomic nuclei that form are often quickly destroyed by these high-energy photons in a process called photodissociation. But about one second after the big bang, high-energy photons become rare due to the expansion and cooling of the universe, allowing helium nuclei to form and remain stable. The universe is now a hot plasma of positively charged hydrogen nuclei (one proton) and helium nuclei (two protons and two neutrons) and negatively charged free electrons.

By three minutes after the big bang, the density of the expanding universe has dropped to the point where particles can no longer get close enough to overcome the Coulomb Barrier and fuse into atomic nuclei. This marks the end of the Nucleosynthesis Epoch. But temperatures are still about one billion K (over sixty times hotter than the center of the sun), which keeps these nuclei ionized, as electrons are still too energetic to stay bound to atomic nuclei and form neutral atoms.

At the end of the Nucleosynthesis Epoch, 75 percent of nucleons are located in hydrogen nuclei, while 25 percent are located in helium nuclei. The measurements of the amount of helium in the current universe closely match these theoretical predictions of primordial abundances from when the universe is just a few minutes old.

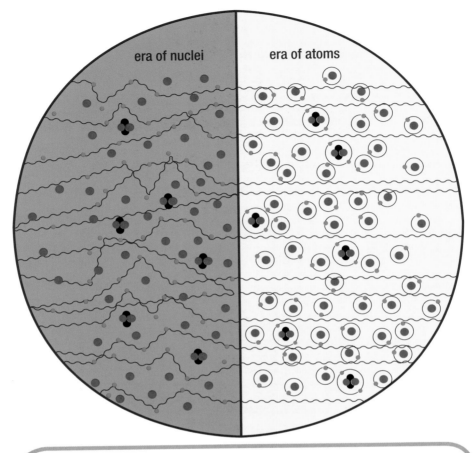

The left panel of this image depicts the Era of Nuclei, when the universe was a plasma of positively charged nuclei and free electrons. The right panel depicts the Era of Atoms, during which electrons combined with nuclei.

Nuclei Epoch

During the Nuclei Epoch, which lasts until the universe is about 380,000 years old, the universe is a plasma of positively charged hydrogen and helium nuclei, negatively charged free electrons, and photons. Free electrons can easily scatter photons of any energy through a process called Thompson scattering. This means that as long as electrons remain free in the universe, photons cannot travel far before being redirected by interactions with these free electrons. This makes the universe opaque to light, similar to the way the sun's plasma is opaque to light: only the light coming from the surface of the sun is visible and not from its deeper layers, because those deeper photons are being redirected by the free electrons in the sun's plasma before they can escape from the sun's surface and travel to the eye.

FIRST LIGHT IN THE UNIVERSE

During the Nuclei Epoch, before neutral atoms formed, the universe was filled with a plasma of positively charged nuclei (protons and neutrons without orbiting electrons) and free electrons (electrons that are not bound to atomic nuclei). During this time, photons could not travel very far without scattering off the free electrons through a process called Thompson scattering. This meant that the universe was opaque to light, similar to a dense fog that obstructs visibility. This is depicted in the left panel of the figure on the previous page, where the free electrons are small blue dots and the interacting photons are the squiggly lines. When the universe was about 380,000 years old, the universe cooled enough for free electrons to combine with the nuclei to form neutral atoms. At this point, photons could travel freely throughout the universe, as shown in the right panel of the figure. These first free photons make up the cosmic microwave background that is still observable today.

The state of the universe drastically changes when the temperature cools to 3000 K (about 5,000°F or 2,760°C, a little less than half the temperature of the surface of the sun). At this temperature, electrons can now combine with nuclei to form neutral atoms that remain stable. At this point, only photons with very specific energies, corresponding to energy transitions within atoms, can interact with matter. This radically lowers the chances that photons and matter will interact, decoupling matter from radiation for the first time in the history of the universe. Matter is now free to cool below the temperatures of the photons, and the photons can travel much more freely throughout space. This makes the universe transparent to light for the first time.

These first free photons from the early universe are still visible today as the cosmic microwave background,[1] which is one of the key pieces of evidence supporting the big bang. But how is light from the past visible today? The reason is the finite speed of light: because light emitted from a source takes time to reach us (rather than arriving instantly), the farther away the source is from us, the further in the past the light was emitted by the time it reaches our eyes. This means that looking far away is like looking backward in time. For example, the sunlight currently hitting Earth's surface was actually emitted from the sun eight minutes in the past! Unfortunately, it is impossible to see the universe before it was 380,000 years old because, as previously discussed, the universe was opaque to light at these earlier times.

Epoch of Atoms & Galaxies

Finally, the universe begins to look a little more familiar. During the Epoch of Atoms, slight density variations in the universe allow gravity to slowly assemble large-scale structures that

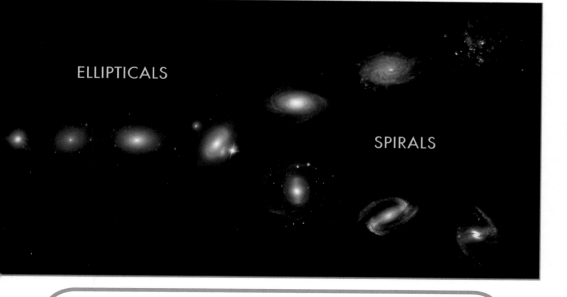

ELLIPTICALS

SPIRALS

This diagram shows Hubble's classification of the different galaxy types by shape.

eventually turn into the first stars. At one billion years old, the first galaxies are formed, marking the end of the Epoch of the Atoms and beginning the Epoch of Galaxies, which continues today. In today's universe, galaxies are common. Galaxies come in different forms and are often divided into two classes: elliptical (at left in the image above) and spiral (right). Hubble thought these different classes were related through an evolutionary sequence.[2] Although galaxies do not actually evolve in this manner, the Hubble sequence is still a nice way to visualize the different types of galaxies.

Chapter Three

Hubble's Expanding Universe

The modern picture of an expanding universe was popularized in the 1920s by an American astronomer named Edwin Hubble (1889–1953).[1] Hubble and his team were measuring distances to other galaxies using the 100-inch (2.54-m) telescope at Mount Wilson Observatory—then the largest telescope in the world (but today optical telescopes can be up to 38.8 feet [10 m] in diameter, and will soon be up to 98.4 feet [30 m] in diameter). At the time, astronomers were not even certain whether other galaxies existed inside or outside of our Milky Way, although now it is accepted that the universe contains roughly one hundred billion galaxies (each with one hundred billion stars). Hubble was able to estimate the distances to other galaxies, showing

The American astronomer Edwin Hubble (1889–1953) is pictured in front of the telescope at the Mount Wilson Observatory that he used to show that the universe is expanding.

that they were indeed located much farther than the confines of our Milky Way. He also measured the motions of these galaxies to show that the farther away a galaxy is from Earth, the faster it is moving away from us. Hubble's finding showed that the universe is not static, but rather expanding, revolutionizing how the universe is understood.

How to Measure the Distances to Galaxies

To measure galactic distances, Hubble used what is known as the inverse-square law, which is illustrated on the next page. This law describes very simply how the apparent brightness of

This image of Cepheid variables in the distant galaxy NGC 4603 was taken by the Hubble Space Telescope (HST).

a star decreases as an observer moves farther and farther away from the star. If the intrinsic brightness of a star is known and it is also possible to measure its apparent brightness, then the distance to the star can be estimated using the inverse square law. In astronomy, standard candles are certain types of stars that always have the same intrinsic brightness, making them valuable tools for measuring distances throughout the universe. In 1924, Hubble used standard candles known as Cepheid variables to measure distances from other galaxies, showing that they were indeed located outside of the Milky Way.

THE INVERSE SQUARE LAW

The intrinsic brightness of a star is how bright the star would be when viewed from right in front of it, while the apparent brightness is how bright the star would appear to be when observing it at some distance. As one moves farther and farther away from the star, it will appear dimmer and dimmer because the starlight is being spread out over larger and larger areas, as shown in the image on the next page. This decreases the star's apparent brightness in a manner that is inversely proportional to the square of its distance, which is why the relation between the intrinsic and apparent brightness of a star is called the inverse square law.

The inverse square law is a powerful tool in astronomy because it can be used to derive distances to other stars and galaxies. For this, astronomers use standard candles, which are special types of bright objects that have known intrinsic brightness. Because their intrinsic brightness is known, one can easily measure their apparent brightness from Earth to derive their distance. Hubble used the inverse square law to show that the universe is expanding.

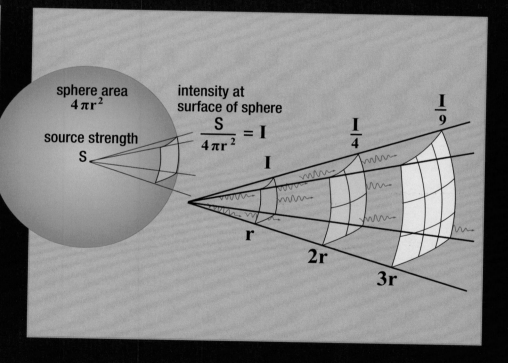

When energy reaches a distance twice as far from its source, it is spread over four times the original area, causing it to have one-fourth the intensity.

How to Measure the Motions of Galaxies

But measuring distances was just the first step in Hubble's landmark discovery of an expanding universe. Around this time, astronomers were also using a phenomenon known as the Doppler effect to measure the movements of distant galaxies relative to Earth. When light is emitted from a source, the light wave has a certain wavelength and frequency. If the source is moving away from Earth, then the waves will be stretched out as they are emitted from the moving source, resulting in longer wavelengths and lower frequencies. This effect is known as redshift because longer wavelengths of light are redder in color in the visible part of the electromagnetic spectrum (the part of the spectrum that can be seen with one's eyes). In the opposite sense, the waves will be squished together if the source is moving toward Earth while it emits light, resulting in shorter wavelengths and higher frequencies. This effect is called blueshift, because shorter wavelengths of light appear bluer in color in the visible spectrum. An everyday

When a source of light, such as a star, moves towards or away from us, its motion changes the way its light appears to us. When a star moves away from us, the light is stretched out, or redshifted. When a star moves towards us, the light is squished together, or blueshifted. Together, the effects of redshift and blueshift are known as the Doppler effect, which is a very powerful tool that astronomers use to study the motions of stars and galaxies. As shown in this figure, astronomers can use the spectra of an object to measure its amount of redshift or blueshift, and thus its motion away from or towards us.

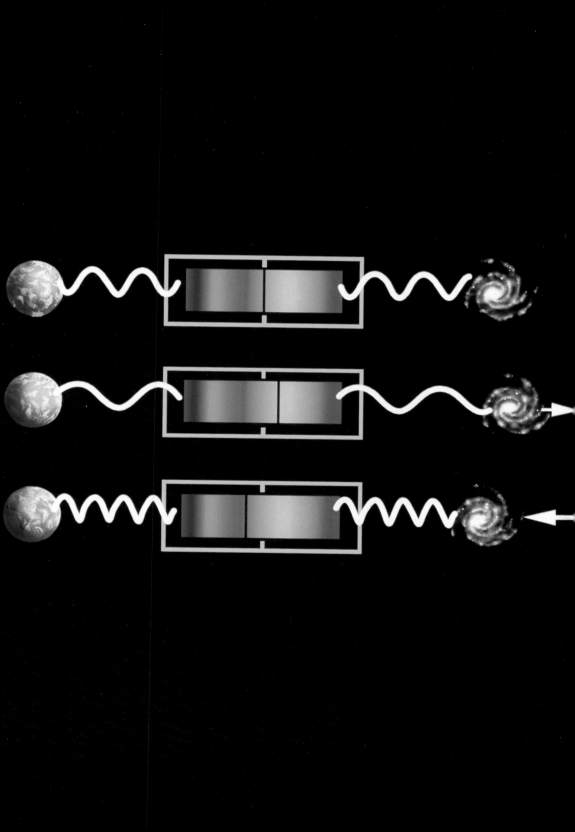

example of Doppler shift is the change in the pitch of a siren as an ambulance drives past you on the street: the higher pitch as the ambulance drives toward you, and the lower pitch as it drives away from you, are both the result of the Doppler effect changing the frequency of the sound waves.

Astronomers can use the magnitude of the redshift or blueshift seen in a star's spectrum to determine the speed at which the star is moving either away from or toward Earth. This quantity is known as the star's radial velocity, where positive radial velocities correspond to stars moving away from Earth, and negative radial velocities correspond to stars moving toward Earth. At the time of Hubble's distance discovery, astronomers expected galaxies to have random motions relative to Earth since Earth was not located in any particularly special place in the universe. In other words, they expected to observe roughly equal numbers of redshifted and blueshifted galaxies with random radial velocities, both negative and positive. But as Hubble began cataloguing the distances and radial velocities of galaxies, he found that most galaxies were not only moving away from Earth in all directions, but also that the magnitude of their redshift was directly proportional to the distance of the galaxy from Earth. In other words, the more distant the galaxy, the faster it is moving away from Earth, implying that the universe is expanding. This can be described with a simple linear relation between distance and radial velocity, now known as Hubble's Law.[2] The constant that connects the two parameters is known as Hubble's constant, often depicted as H_0.

The implications of Hubble's law revolutionized how the universe was viewed: the universe was no longer static, but rather expanding in all directions! Although Hubble's original finding was based on a small sample of galaxies and used distance methods that turned out to be partially incorrect, Hubble's law has been refined over the years, and the linear relationship between the distance and radial velocity of nearby galaxies remains valid today.

It is important to note that the fact that other galaxies appear to be moving away from Earth in all directions does *not* mean that Earth is at the center of the universe. Rather, in an expanding universe, the view from all galaxies should show all other galaxies moving away in all directions. A common analogy is a rising loaf of raisin bread: as the bread expands during baking, all of the raisins move farther and farther apart from each other, and any given raisin will see all other raisins moving away from it, no matter where it is located in the loaf.

Chapter Four

Observational Evidence for the Big Bang

Scientific theories are models of nature, and any good scientific model should make predictions that can be confirmed with observation and experimentation. At first, it may seem impossible that a model of the first fractions of a second of the universe can be tested under the very different conditions that exist today. However, one of the reasons why the big bang theory is so widely accepted is that it makes clear predictions about the present state of the universe, which can be tested with astronomical observations by simply looking up at the night sky, or even just turning on the television.

The Cosmic Microwave Background: Big Bang Archaeology

One key implication of the big bang is that the universe should look more or less the same in every direction, at least on very large scales. And indeed, when looking across the universe at very distant galaxies, there is more or less the same distribution of matter in all directions. More significantly, this homogeneity is clearly imprinted on something called the cosmic microwave background (CMB).

The big bang theory predicts that as the universe expanded, it also cooled. At the end of the Nuclei Epoch, the universe had cooled to the point where electrons could combine with nuclei to form neutral atoms, allowing photons to travel freely across the universe for the first time. At this point, the universe became transparent to light, but due to the finite speed of light, these first free photons from the very distant reaches of the universe are only now arriving to Earth. Moreover, because the expansion of the universe has greatly redshifted these photons, they appear as microwave radiation corresponding to chilly temperatures of only 3 K (-454°F or -270°C) rather than their original 3,000 K (approximately 4,940°F or 2,727°C). This leftover radiation from the early universe is known as the CMB.

In the mid-1960s, two physicists at Princeton University, Bob Dicke (1916–1997) and Jim Peebles (1935–), were working on the theory of the CMB and setting out to detect it.[1] As it happens, two other physicists at Bell Laboratories in New Jersey, Arno Penzias (1933–) and Robert Wilson (1936–), had already accidentally discovered the CMB while attempting to calibrate a very sensitive microwave antenna. Penzias and Wilson, much to their annoyance, were finding an unceasing background noise in their observations, which appeared to come from every direction in the sky, no matter where they pointed their antenna, or at what time of day or night. The fact that the radiation was the same no matter the direction implied that it was coming from outside

Nobel Prize winners Penzias and Wilson are pictured with the microwave antenna they used to discover the cosmic microwave background (CMB).

of Earth, whereas the indifference to time of day implied that it came from outside the solar system and even from beyond the galaxy. This is because if the signal came from a specific point in the sky, it should appear and disappear in cyclic patterns as Earth rotates on its axis and orbits around the sun.

The story goes that Penzias and Wilson initially thought that the noise came from pigeon droppings that they discovered on their antenna, yet the static persisted even after a good cleaning. Fortunately, Penzias and Wilson soon heard of the work of Dicke and Peebles, realizing that their background noise fit the exact description of the CMB—they had accidentally found the remnants of the big bang. For their observational discovery, Penzias and Wilson were awarded the Nobel Prize for Physics in 1978, but unfortunately Dicke and Peebles were not included.

For a closer look at the CMB, scientists have launched three important space missions since its discovery.[2] The Cosmic Microwave Background Explorer (COBE) was launched in the early 1990s to test the idea that the CMB should have a perfect thermal spectrum representing the heat of the early universe, but redshifted (or cooled) by a factor of one thousand due to the subsequent expansion of the universe. The results of COBE showed that the CMB did indeed have a perfect thermal spectrum, corresponding to a frigid temperature of 2.73 K (-454°F or -270°C), providing substantial support for the big bang theory.

NASA later launched the Wilkinson Microwave Anisotropy Probe (WMAP) in 2001 to map in great detail the temperature variations in the CMB. WMAP showed that the CMB is largely homogenous, as expected, but also that there were small temperature variations representing the slight density

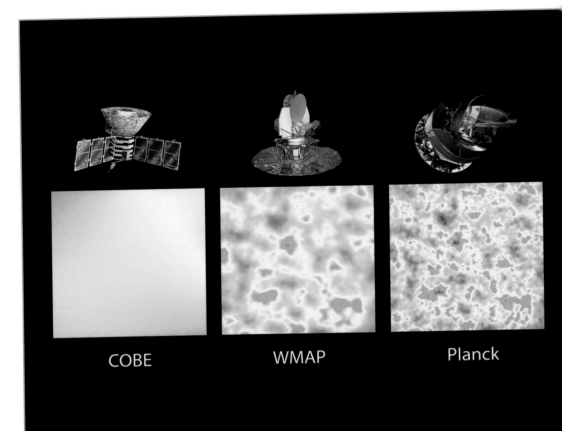

COBE   WMAP   Planck

Three space missions—COBE, WMAP, and Planck—have been launched over the past several decades to study the CMB in increasingly great detail, as shown in the bottom panels. The color variations in the images reflect tiny temperature differences in the CMB that are on the order of just one part in 100,000.

enhancements that are needed to explain the eventual formation of the galaxies seen today. In 2009, the European Space Agency also launched the Planck mission to obtain even higher resolution observations of the CMB at multiple wavelengths. Scientists have used the data collected by Planck to greatly improve how the universe is understood, such as by placing the strongest constraints on the age of the universe (13.799 ± 0.038 years) and the fraction of the universe that is made up of dark energy and dark matter.

However, it is possible to see the CMB even without expensive equipment! Anyone can see the CMB on an antenna-fed television: if one tunes the television to a station between programmed channels, the static observed on the screen is about 1 percent CMB radiation (though unfortunately this does not work for more modern cable or satellite televisions).

Helium Abundance in the Current Universe

Another important observational confirmation of the big bang is the abundance of helium in the universe. About 25 percent of matter appears to be in the form of helium. This substantial and near-uniform helium abundance across the universe means that helium must have formed very early in the history of the universe, when conditions were sufficiently hot and dense for hydrogen to fuse into helium. Otherwise, only the very small amount of helium that has been able to form in the center of stars would be visible. Indeed, calculations show that only a small percentage of the current helium in the universe could have formed from stellar nucleosynthesis.

The big bang theory predicts that this primordial helium was formed during the Nucleosynthesis Epoch. During this time, the universe was only about one minute old, and it was filled with matter particles (protons, neutrons, electrons, and neutrinos) and photons. Importantly, protons outnumbered neutrons by seven to one at this time. This is because very early in the Nucleosynthesis Epoch, when temperatures were extremely high and energy was readily available, neutrons and protons could easily convert back and forth and were therefore in equal numbers. But when temperatures fell below approximately 10^{11} K, the fact that neutrons are slightly more massive than protons meant that the energy needed for converting protons to neutrons (according to $E = mc^2$) was no longer available. Thus neutrons could turn into protons, but protons could not turn back into neutrons, resulting in an over-abundance of protons.

"EUREKA"

Edgar Allan Poe, in his 1848 essay "Eureka," postulated why the night sky is dark despite the vast number of stars in the universe, somewhat anticipating the future quantitative solutions to Olbers' Paradox:

Were the succession of stars endless, then the background of the sky would present us a uniform luminosity, like that displayed by the Galaxy—since there could be absolutely no point, in all

(continued on page 44)

Copyright 1904
C.T. Talman.

The American author Edgar Allan Poe anticipated Olbers'
Paradox in his essay "Eureka."

(continued from page 42)

that background, at which would not exist a star. The only mode, therefore, in which, under such a state of affairs, we could comprehend the voids which our telescopes find in innumerable directions, would be by supposing the distance of the invisible background so immense that no ray from it has yet been able to reach us at all.

As the universe continued to cool over the Nucleosynthesis Epoch, helium nuclei formed and remained stable, as high-energy gamma rays were now relatively rare. The big bang theory predicts that all of the available neutrons should have become incorporated into helium nuclei. Given the seven-to-one ratio of protons to neutrons, this should produce a mass ratio of 25 percent helium and 75 percent hydrogen at the end of the Nucleosynthesis Epoch. This is exactly what is seen today, providing another big win for the big bang theory.

The formation of heavier elements, such as carbon and oxygen, did not occur in the early universe. This is because by the time stable helium nuclei (the building blocks of heavier nuclei) had formed, the temperatures and densities of the expanding universe had already dropped to values that were too low to build anything heavier than helium. The heavier elements were instead formed later, during nuclear fusion in the centers of stars, a process that continues today.

Olbers' Paradox: Why Is the Night Sky Dark?

Before the development of the big bang theory, it was commonly assumed that the universe was static and infinite in both space and time. However, if this were true, the night sky would not be dark, because every direction would have a line-of-sight that ended in a star. This is analogous to being inside a forest that is so large and dense that, no matter where one looks, only trees are visible. Although the more distant stars would be fainter, one would also see more of them within a given area of sky. Calculations show that this would result in a night sky as bright as the surface of a star, rather than the darkness seen each night.

This issue is commonly referred to as Olbers' Paradox, named after the German astronomer Heinrich Olbers (1758–1840), who articulated the problem in the 1820s. As with many namesakes in astronomy, Olbers was not the first to come up with this idea (Johannes Kepler may have done so in the early 1600s), and he also did not contribute much to its solution (some say Lord Kelvin was the first to put forth a quantitative resolution in 1901).

Nevertheless, the fact that the night sky is dark suggests that either the universe is nonstatic or that it is finite in time or space. The big bang provides a possible solution to Olbers' paradox by giving the universe a beginning and thus a particular age. When combined with the finite speed of light, a finite age means that we can only see the stars close enough that their light has had sufficient time to reach Earth. Because the density of stars within this observable volume is sufficiently low, the view from Earth out into the universe mostly avoids

ending in a star. Interestingly, the American writer Edgar Allan Poe put forth a qualitative version of this explanation in his 1848 essay "Eureka." Additionally, according to the big bang theory, the universe is not static but rather expanding, and at faster speeds for more distant stars. This means that any light emitted during the very early times of the universe, such as the CMB, will be redshifted to substantially longer wavelengths, thereby no longer contributing to the visual light visible to the eye.

The big bang theory helps explain why the night sky appears to be dark instead of as bright as the surface of a star.

Chapter Five

Related Issues in Cosmology

The basic eras of the big bang are well established and have been tested with observations of the current universe with great success. Nevertheless, ongoing discoveries in the field of cosmology continue to unveil new and interesting features of the universe, such as the presence of dark matter and dark energy. Although some of these aspects remain debated, they can enrich the story of the big bang in many ways. They may also help to explain the ultimate fate of the universe.

Dark Matter

All of the matter in the universe visible today—including you, your socks, and all the planets, stars, and galaxies—is made of normal matter. Although normal matter makes up everything that is interacted with on a daily basis, it actually accounts for only about 5 percent of all the matter in the universe. The rest of the matter is in the form of dark matter and dark energy.[1]

Astronomers know that dark matter exists because of its gravitational influence on normal matter. In other words, because dark matter has mass, it can change the motions of normal matter through its gravitational force. It is then possible to use those changes in the motion of normal matter to infer that dark matter must exist, even though it cannot be directly observed.

This was first discovered when looking at the speeds of stars orbiting in spiral galaxies, such as the Milky Way. The speed at which a star orbits in a galaxy depends on its distance from the center of the galaxy, and also on the mass of the galaxy inside the star's orbit. In an idealized case (meaning circular orbits and centrally concentrated mass), this is just Kepler's third law. If all of the matter in a galaxy were normal matter, then the mass of the galaxy could be estimated from the number of stars seen, and then the motions of those stars could be predicted based on their distance from the galaxy's center. However, when astronomers measured the motions of stars in galaxies, they found that the stellar motions were not what they expected. Instead, they discovered that the unexpected stellar motions could be explained by a lot of extra "dark" mass in the outer regions of galaxies, which was not being accounted for by observations of just the normal matter.

Although dark matter is not directly visible, scientists are confident that dark matter exists because of their robust understanding of gravity. The big remaining mystery of dark matter, however, is exactly what it could be made of. Some of the dark matter is likely just normal matter that is not emitting brightly enough to be detected from Earth, such as faint brown dwarf stars and free-floating planets, which are collectively called

MACHOS (Massive Compact Halo Objects). But most dark matter may actually be in the form of weakly interacting particles that are currently unknown. These WIMPS (Weakly Interactive Massive Particles) are thought to be very hard to detect because they do not emit or absorb light, and also do not interact or exchange energy with normal matter.

Dark Energy

Despite their similar names, dark energy and dark matter are very different. Dark energy is believed to be an energy field that permeates all of space. As the universe expands, dark energy fills the expanding space, thereby increasing its strength. Because dark energy has a repulsive effect, its increasing strength serves to accelerate the expansion of the universe. Scientists are still trying to understand dark energy, and they do not yet have a good theory on what it might be. However, there is an increasing amount of theoretical and observational evidence supporting the existence of dark energy.

EVIDENCE FOR DARK MATTER

According to Kepler's third law, the speed at which an object orbits a much more massive central body should decline with its distance from that central body. This is exactly what is seen in the solar system: the closest planet, Mercury, orbits very quickly around the sun, while planets farther out, such as Uranus and Neptune, orbit much more slowly around the sun. This so-called Keplerian motion is shown by the blue line in the figure. If dark matter did not exist, then there would be the same drop in the rotational speeds of stars in the outer regions of galaxies. However, instead there are flat rotation curves, as shown for the Milky Way by the yellow line in the figure. This flattening of galaxy rotation curves implies that there is a lot of mass in the outer regions of galaxies that is not being accounted for by normal matter. Because we cannot see this matter (since it does not emit or absorb light), we call it dark matter.

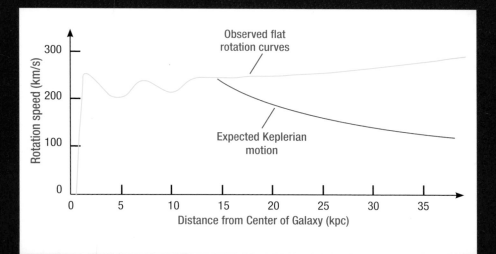

The fact that flat galaxy rotation curves are observed (as indicated by the yellow line) instead of the declining rotation curves predicted by Kepler's third law (indicated by the blue line) suggests that dark matter exists in the outer regions of galaxies.

In particular, the 2011 Nobel Prize in Physics was awarded for the observational confirmation of the accelerating expansion of the universe—a key piece of evidence supporting the existence of dark energy. Physicists Saul Perlmutter (1959–), Brian Schmidt (1967–), and Adam Riess (1969–) were jointly awarded the Nobel Prize for their leadership in the discovery. To understand their method, recall Hubble's story from Chapter 3: Hubble used

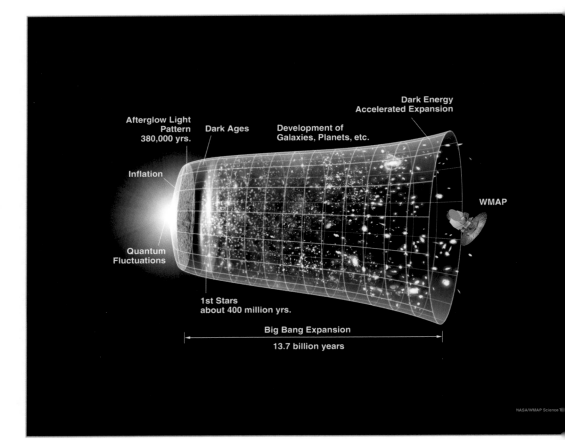

This diagram demonstrates the expansion of the universe over cosmic time.

standard candles to measure distances to galaxies by comparing their apparent brightness to their intrinsic brightness, which allowed him to show that the universe is expanding at a constant rate. Perlmutter, Schmidt, and Riess showed that this is actually only true for nearby galaxies, and that more distant galaxies are moving away from Earth at faster rates than predicted by Hubble's Law. To show this, they used Type Ia ("one-A") supernovae, which are exceptionally bright exploding stars that can be used as standard candles in very distant galaxies. They measured the apparent brightness of these supernovae in galaxies that are at known distances across the universe. When comparing their measurements to the expected apparent brightness based on Hubble's constantly expanding universe, they found that the most distant supernovae were fainter than expected. This is a sign that the universe is accelerating its expansion, carrying these distant objects much farther away than predicted by Hubble's Law.

Inflation

The freezing out of the strong nuclear force at the end of the GUT Epoch may have released an enormous amount of energy, triggering an event called inflation, during which the universe expanded from the size of an atomic nucleus to the size of the solar system in just 10^{-36} seconds. Although this sounds strange, inflation explains some of the most important observational features of the current universe. Observations of the current universe are the only way that one can test inflation, as the densities and temperatures in the early universe were too extreme to be re-created in today's laboratories.

The *Planck* mission produced an all-sky picture of the infant universe from its observations.

Inflation is one of the best explanations for the smoothness of the CMB temperature structure. Observations from space missions like COBE, WMAP, and Planck showed that the temperature fluctuations in the CMB typically deviate from the average by only one part in 100,000.[2] In other words, the temperature of the universe is nearly uniform no matter where you look, at least over large scales. The uniformity of the CMB is interesting because it means that at some point in the past, every point in the universe was close enough to exchange energy and therefore equalized temperatures. When inflation occurred, the universe expanded rapidly, but each part of the universe remembered this shared temperature despite now being separated by incredibly great scales. This resulted in the smoothness of the CMB observable today.

Closer inspection of the figure on the previous page shows that although the CMB appears very smooth over large scales, there are also clear structures on very small scales (the bluer or redder regions in the figure). These small variations, known as anisotropies, correspond to areas of increased or decreased temperature and thus density in the early universe. Gravitational attraction of the over-dense regions caused them to grow into even larger density enhancements, which then continued to grow over billions of years into the stars, galaxies, and galaxy clusters that are seen today.

But where did these anisotropies come from in the first place? Inflation, combined with quantum mechanics, can explain their origin better than any other cosmological theory that is currently available. Quantum mechanics states that on very small scales (smaller than the size of an atom) the energy field at any point in space is constantly fluctuating, resulting in tiny quantum "ripples" in the energy field throughout the universe. These quantum ripples are themselves much too small to explain the anisotropies observed in the CMB. However, inflation would have stretched out these tiny quantum fluctuations, from scales of smaller than an atomic nucleus to sizes comparable to the solar system, enabling their eventual growth into the large-scale structures that are seen in today's universe. This is a remarkable statement, as it implies that all of the stars and galaxies in the current universe originated as just tiny quantum fluctuations when the universe was the size of an atomic nucleus!

Chapter Six

The Fate of the Universe

Although the big bang theory mostly focuses on the beginnings of the universe, it can also help explain how the universe might end. Hubble's work showed that the universe is expanding, but the universe is full of matter, such as all the stars and galaxies, which are attracted to each other by gravity. This gravitational attraction of matter fights against the expansion of the universe, which means that if the gravitational attraction of matter is strong enough, it could slow down or even reverse the expansion of the universe. As a result, the ultimate fate of the universe depends on its total density compared to the momentum of its expansion. This is a consequence of Einstein's theory of general relativity, which demonstrates that the gravitational effect of matter can curve the surrounding space.

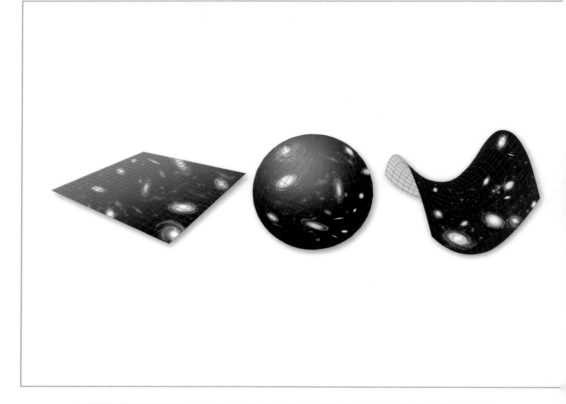

The different possible geometries of the universe are flat (*left*), closed (*middle*), and open (*right*).

Big Crunch or Big Freeze?

The different possibilities for the future of the universe are often made by analogy to three-dimensional shapes that can be more easily visualized.[1] If the universe is at critical density, then the gravitational pull of matter exactly matches the momentum of the universe's expansion. This is described as a geometrically "flat" universe, in which the expansion is halted after an infinite amount of time (left panel of figure on the previous page). If the density of matter in the universe is above the critical density, then gravity would eventually win, slowly halting and ultimately collapsing the universe back in on itself in a "Big Crunch." This type of universe is known as a "closed" universe because the geometry of space would be analogous to the surface of a closed sphere (middle panel). If instead the density of matter in the universe were below the critical density, then the gravitational attraction of matter would be insufficient to stop the outward expansion of the universe, resulting in a universe that continues to expand and cool forever in a "Big Freeze." This is called an "open" universe because the geometry of space would be analogous to the shape of an open saddle (right panel).

The critical density is incredibly small—only about 10^{-29} grams per cubic centimeter—which is roughly equivalent to a measly six protons per cubic meter. Observations show that normal matter only accounts for about 5 percent of the matter density required to halt the expansion of the universe. The amount of dark matter in the universe can then be added to see if it can make up the missing mass to reach the critical density. However, studies of the motions of galaxies and galaxy clusters suggest that dark matter only makes up about 26 percent of the critical density. Thus it seems that the universe is set to end in a "Big Freeze," in which it continues to expand and cool forever.

A Flat and Accelerating Universe?

Results from the WMAP mission showed that the universe is spatially flat to within 1 percent, which means that the universe is at the critical density. This implies that the universe, for some reason, is perfectly balanced between two extreme outcomes of a closed or open universe: even small deviations from the critical density would have resulted in a drastically different universe today, either having already collapsed back in on itself or expanded too quickly for galaxies to ever have formed. Why should the universe be "fine-tuned" to the critical density, when it could have had any other value? And where is the 69 percent of this critical density that could not be accounted for by normal matter and dark matter?

These questions can be answered by the combination of inflation and dark energy. Inflation can explain why the universe appears flat because of the effects of such rapid and dramatic expansion on the geometry of the universe. These geometrical effects are similar to the flattening of a balloon's surface as it is being inflated with air: as the balloon gets inflated, the surface appears increasingly flat to a small observer on its surface. This also explains why the universe appears to be "fine-tuned" to the critical density: it does not matter what the curvature of the universe was prior to inflation, because the event of inflation would always produce an overall geometry of the universe that appears to be nearly perfectly flat.

But if the universe is flat, then it must also be at the critical density. The combination of normal matter and dark matter only accounts for about 31 percent of the critical density, so where is the rest of it? The answer may be in dark energy (recall that energy and mass are interchangeable by Einstein's $E=mc^2$). Remarkably, the supernovae observations that revealed the accelerating expansion of the universe also showed that the strength of the required repulsive force was roughly equal to the amount needed to make the universe reach critical density, when combined with normal matter and dark matter.

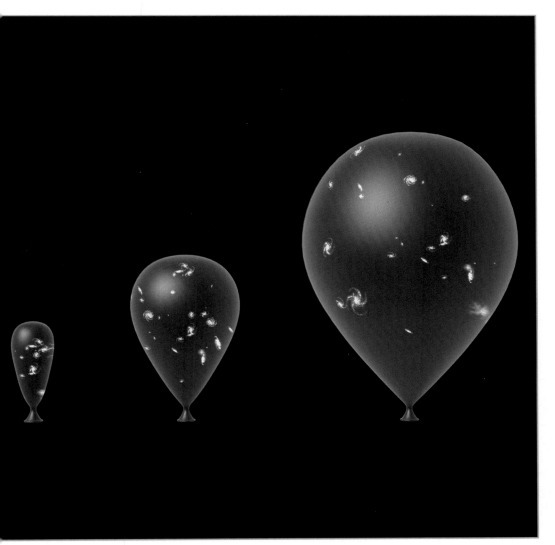

To a small observer standing on a balloon, the observable surface appears increasingly flat as the balloon is blown up. This is a useful analogy for understanding how cosmic inflation made the observable universe appear geometrically flat. Because the universe expanded so dramatically during inflation, any curvature is no longer noticeable within the observable universe, making it appear very flat. This also explains why the universe appears to be "fine-tuned" to the critical density.

These results also imply that dark energy actually makes up the majority of the matter density in the universe (69 percent). Recalling that dark energy is associated with a repulsive force causing the accelerated expansion of the universe, this implies that the ultimate fate of the universe will be an accelerated version of the "Big Freeze" scenario. As such, regardless of whether dark energy exists, it appears that the universe is destined to expand forever, with galaxies receding farther and farther away from each other over time, as space cools to icier and icier temperatures.

THE LASER INTERFEROMETER GRAVITATIONAL-WAVE OBSERVATORY

The Laser Interferometer Gravitational-Wave Observatory (LIGO) is a large-scale physics observatory designed to detect gravitational waves.[2] Gravitational waves are ripples in space-time generated by gravitational interactions between massive objects, and they are a key prediction of Einstein's theory of general relativity. LIGO consists of two facilities in the United States, one near Hanford, Washington, and another near Livingston, Louisiana. Each facility is

This LIGO facility is located in Hanford, Washington. The other is in Livingston, Louisiana.

a laser interferometer that can detect extremely small distortions in space-time resulting from the passage of gravitational waves through Earth. The interferometers are L-shaped, with two arms that are each 2.5 miles (4 km) long. Lasers are beamed down the arms and bounced back via mirrors, providing extremely sensitive rulers that are capable of measuring distortions of just one ten-thousandth the diameter of a proton! Having two LIGO facilities operating simultaneously in different parts of the country acts as a check to rule out false-positive signals (signals that are not actually due to gravitational waves from an event in space, but rather a

(continued on the next page)

(continued from the previous page)

Two black holes merge and form gravitational waves that ripple outward.

local disturbance of terrestrial origin); if an event is truly a gravitational wave, both facilities should detect it. The image above shows an illustration of two black holes merging and the gravitational waves that ripple outward as the black holes spiral toward each other. The first observations of gravitational waves were made by LIGO on September 14, 2015, with the signals matching predictions of general relativity for the merger of a pair of black holes that were twenty-nine and thirty-six times the mass of the sun.

What Will the End Look Like?

There is a growing consensus among scientists that the universe will expand forever, regardless of the ongoing discussions about dark energy. So, it is worth asking, what will happen to all the stars, galaxies, and planets in a universe that is forever expanding?

In the current universe, gas and dust in the interstellar and intergalactic medium are actively being turned into stars. These stars eventually end their lives as remnant white dwarfs, neutron stars, or black holes. During the end stages of a star's lifetime, some of its material is ejected back into space to enrich the next generation of stars. However, most of the material remains "locked" in these stellar remnants. Because not all of the stellar material is recycled, eventually more and more of it will be locked into stellar remnants until there is no more material left to form new stars. In about one trillion years, due to the (possibly accelerating) expansion of the universe, vast distances will separate galaxies, and all of the stars will have died out. The universe will fade to darkness.

After stars have stopped forming, the main events will be the collisions of stellar remnants. Because of the vast distances between such objects, these events will be incredibly rare. For example, the probability of the sun (or its remnant white dwarf) colliding with another star is only expected to happen once every 10^{15} years (recall that our galaxy is only on the order of 10^9 years old). Nevertheless, these events do happen in today's universe. Recently, the collisions of remnant black holes and neutron stars have been detected by LIGO via the resulting gravitational waves, giving insight into these special events.

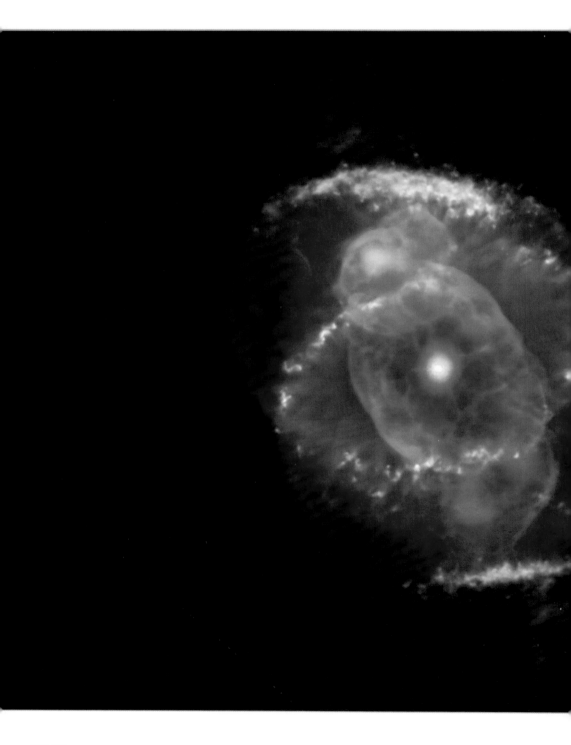

Some of these stellar remnants, as well as rogue planets, will fall into the black holes at the centers of their galaxies, while others will be ejected from their galaxies to become free-floating objects. This means that, eventually, the universe will only consist of extremely super-massive black holes and lonely scattered dead stars or orphaned planets. These objects will continue to recede away from each other, while temperatures in the universe asymptotically approach zero.

According to GUT, even protons will eventually fall apart. The half-life of a proton is at least 10^{32} years, which is an unimaginably long time. But, if protons do decay, by

White dwarfs, like the one at the center of this image of a planetary nebula, are one type of stellar remnant.

the time the universe is 10^{40} years old, all atomic matter will have disintegrated into radiation and subatomic particles, such as electrons and neutrinos. Even black holes may eventually evaporate as their mass-energy turns into radiation. The largest black holes will stick around the longest, but by 10^{100} years even the largest black holes (possibly of one trillion solar masses) will have evaporated. Then the universe will consist of only photons and subatomic particles, separated by such enormous distances that they will never interact.

Looking Ahead

The theory of the beginnings of the universe, known as the big bang theory, is well founded on strong understandings of fundamental physics. Observations of the current universe also allow one to successfully test predictions of the big bang, such as the presence and characteristics of the cosmic microwave background, making it a widely accepted theory by modern cosmologists.

However, some unknowns remain, such as the extreme physical conditions of the very initial moments of the universe during the Planck Epoch, when the universe had nearly infinite densities and temperatures. Solving these unknowns will ultimately require joining quantum mechanisms and general relativity into a single unified theory called quantum gravity, which has yet to be done. Additionally, there is building evidence for dark energy, with observations that the universe is accelerating its expansion and also at the critical density. Yet despite the major implications of dark energy for the history and future of the universe, its fundamental nature remains one of the foremost mysteries in cosmology.

Looking ahead, ongoing advances in both theory and observation keep pushing the understanding of the universe forward. For example, the first direct detections of gravitational waves by LIGO are giving new insights into the collisions of massive stellar remnants like black holes and neutron stars— these collisions will eventually be the dominant events in a big bang universe, which appears destined to expand forever.

CHAPTER NOTES

Chapter One
The Beginning of the Beginning

1. "Max Planck: Originator of Quantum Theory," *European Space Agency*, accessed November 30, 2017, http://www.esa.int/Our_Activities/Space_Science/Planck/Max_Planck_Originator_of_quantum_theory.
2. Mark O. Kimball and Eric Silk, "Temperature Scales and Absolute Zero," *Goddard Space Flight Center,* September 11, 2014, https://cryo.gsfc.nasa.gov/introduction/temp_scales.html.

Chapter Two
From Protons to Galaxies

1. Britt Griswold and Edward J. Wollack, "Tests of the Big Bang: The CMB," *NASA*, May 9, 2016, https://wmap.gsfc.nasa.gov/universe/bb_tests_cmb.html.
2. "The Hubble Tuning Fork," Hubble *Space Telescope*, accessed November 30, 2017, https://www.spacetelescope.org/images/heic9902o/.

Chapter Three
Hubble's Expanding Universe

1. Phil Newman and J.D. Myers, "Edwin P. Hubble," *NASA,* February 2, 2012, https://asd.gsfc.nasa.gov/archive/hubble/overview/hubble_bio.html.

2. Barbara Mattson and J.D. Myers, "Using Hubble's Law," *Goddard Space Flight Center*, May 5, 2016, https://imagine.gsfc.nasa.gov/features/yba/M31_velocity/hubble_law/index.html.

Chapter Four
Observational Evidence for the Big Bang

1. "Cosmic Microwave Background Radiation," *Nokia Bell Labs*, accessed November 30, 2017, https://www.bell-labs.com/explore/stories-changed-world/Cosmic-Microwave-Background-Discovery/.
2. "The Big Bang," *NASA Science Beta,* accessed November 30, 2017, https://science.nasa.gov/astrophysics/focus-areas/what-powered-the-big-bang.

Chapter Five
Related Issues in Cosmology

1. Britt Griswold and Edward J. Wollack, "What is the Universe Made of?" *NASA*, January 24, 2014, https://map.gsfc.nasa.gov/universe/uni_matter.html.
2. "Planck Science Team Home," *European Space Agency*, accessed November 30, 2017, https://www.cosmos.esa.int/web/planck.

Chapter Six
The Fate of the Universe

1. Britt Griswold and Edward J. Wollack, "Will the Universe Expand Forever?" *NASA,* January 24, 2014, https://map.gsfc.nasa.gov/universe/uni_shape.html.
2. "What is LIGO?" *LIGO Caltech*, accessed November 30, 2017, https://www.ligo.caltech.edu/page/what-is-ligo.

GLOSSARY

anisotropies Small temperature variations in the thermal radiation left over from the big bang, known as the cosmic microwave background.

annihilation The process of a particle and its antiparticle colliding, converting their mass energy entirely into two photons known as gamma rays.

antiparticle An exact copy of a particle, except with opposite electric charge.

apparent brightness The brightness of an object as it appears to an observer that is some distance away from the object due to the geometrical dilution of light.

beta decay The type of radioactive decay that is governed by the weak nuclear force.

cosmic microwave background The remnant light from the early universe, now greatly redshifted to microwave wavelengths.

Coulomb barrier The energy barrier that exists due to the electromagnetic force, which two nucleons must overcome in order to get close enough to undergo nuclear fusion.

critical density The density of the universe at which the gravitational pull of matter exactly matches the momentum of the universe's expansion, resulting in a geometrically flat universe.

dark energy An energy field with a repulsive effect that permeates all of space and may be causing the accelerated expansion of the universe.

dark matter The matter whose presence is inferred from its gravitational influence on normal matter, since it does not emit or absorb light.

Doppler effect The apparent change in the frequency and wavelength of a wave to an observer that is moving relative to the source of the wave.

free electrons Electrons that are not bound to atomic nuclei.

gamma ray A very high-energy photon produced during collisions of elementary particles.

Hubble's constant The rate of universal expansion as first estimated by Edwin Hubble.

inflation The extremely dramatic and rapid expansion of the early universe, which can be used to explain many important observable features of the current universe.

intrinsic brightness The brightness of a source, independent of its distance from an observer.

inverse-square law The physical law stating that the apparent brightness of a source is inversely proportional to the square of the distance of the source from the observer.

nucleosynthesis The formation of atomic nuclei from protons and neutrons.

nucleus The central part of an atom consisting of only protons and neutrons (collectively known as nucleons), held together by the strong force.

photodissociation The decomposition of a nuclei, atoms, or molecules by photons.

photon A massless packet of light with a specific wavelength and frequency.

plasma Ionized matter consisting of positively charged nuclei and free electrons.

radial velocity The speed of an object moving in the direction directly away from an observer.

redshift The stretching of the wavelengths of light from a source that is moving away as a result of the Doppler effect.

spectrum The light from a source split into its component wavelengths.

standard candles Special classes of astronomical objects that have the same intrinsic brightness and are therefore useful for determining distances across the universe.

Thompson scattering The scattering of a photon off a free charged particle, such as an electron.

FURTHER READING

Books

Blumenthal, Kelly. *Cosmic Inflation Explained*. New York, NY: Enslow Publishing, 2018.

deGrasse Tyson, Neil. *Astrophysics for People in a Hurry*. New York, NY: W. W. Norton & Company, 2017.

deGrasse Tyson, Neil. *Death by Black Hole: And Other Cosmic Quandaries*. New York, NY: W. W. Norton & Company, 2014.

Hawking, Stephen. *A Brief History of Time: From the Big Bang to Black Holes*. New York, NY: Bantam Books, 1988.

Negus, James. *Black Holes Explained*. New York, NY: Enslow Publishing, 2018.

Pamplona, Alberto H. *A Visual Guide to the Universe*. New York, NY: Rosen Publishing, 2017.

Scott, Elaine. *Space, Stars, and the Beginning of Time: What the Hubble Telescope Saw*. Boston, MA: Clarion Books, 2011.

Websites

Explore NASA Science

science.nasa.gov/

NASA's Science Mission Directorate website for learning about current NASA missions and programs related to the big bang.

Planck Science Team Home

www.cosmos.esa.int/web/planck

The European Space Agency's official website for the *Planck* mission explaining the mission's contributions to the understanding of the big bang and other issues in cosmology.

Wilkinson Microwave Anisotropy Probe

map.gsfc.nasa.gov/

NASA's mission website for WMAP, with information about the mission's contributions to the understanding of the big bang and other issues in cosmology.

INDEX